T0197336

LOVE & WISDOM

LOVE & WISDOM

Understand Why "Me, Myself, &
I" Comes Before "You & I"

JENNIFER ABRAHAMS

authorHOUSE®

AuthorHouse™ UK
1663 Liberty Drive
Bloomington, IN 47403 USA
www.authorhouse.co.uk
Phone: 0800.197.4150

Published by AuthorHouse 03/03/2015

ISBN: 978-1-4969-9381-6 (sc)
ISBN: 978-1-4969-9382-3 (hc)
ISBN: 978-1-4969-9383-0 (e)

Print information available on the last page.

Contents

Acknowledgements

I want to thank my sweet and precious mother, Deborah Oluyemisi Alexis, for all of your love, prayers, encouragement and tremendous support as I wrote this book. I simply could not have done this without you. You're my best friend. I love you, mummy.

I want to thank my hardworking and focused father, Peter Abrahams. You're my inspiration, mentor and friend. You showed me that hard work pays off when you choose not to give up. Thank you Dad, you lead me to success through your examples. I truly appreciate and love you.

I want to thank Prophet Bonito in Jamaica for speaking this book into existence when I felt like giving up on it.

I want to thank Minister Abay Aromire, whom I affectionately call Dad for encouraging me to change my reality for the better.

I want to thank my friend, Topsy Balogun, for supporting me in so many valuable ways as I wrote this book. I also want to thank my uncle, Mr Robert Opara, for being a tremendous financial blessing towards the actualization of this book. Thanks for having my back.

And I want to thank Michelle Jane for all of her hard and efficient work that made this book a reality and a success.

I appreciate you all and thank you truly.

Why I Wrote This Book:
Marriage Mathematics

There is nothing more valuable, precious, or prized in this thing called life than having a genuine friendship with a genuine friend. Platinum, white gold, yellow gold, rose gold, silver, diamonds, rubies, sapphires, oil, gas, coal, iron, copper, the British pound, the American dollar, or the Chinese yuan – none of these things are terribly valuable when compared to an authentic friendship with an authentic friend. Genuine friendship is the ultimate gift.

Friendship can involve several people, but there is an exclusivity with two friends that surpasses all other types of friendship. This exclusive, ultimate level of friendship is called *marriage*. Friendship doesn't get any friendlier than marriage because marriage is the friendship of friendships.

Friendship Doesn't Get Any Friendlier Than Marriage

Marriage is the ultimate bond of friendship because it has its own mathematics. Yes, marriage *is* mathematics. It's the only level of friendship that results in a mathematical equation of two people – one man and one woman – becoming *one*. Marriage, in essence, is one thing and one thing only: a disposition. One's disposition is made up of the inherent qualities of one's mind and character. In other words, we can basically say that marriage is the mathematical equation of one man's disposition being added to one woman's disposition in order to equal one dispositional unit. And that unit can build a life together in an exclusive partnership.

Why You Comes before Us

When you think about marriage, I'm sure that one of the most (if not the most) important factor that comes to mind is the person that you will marry. During this thought process, I'm sure that you have a few questions flowing through your mind: *What will he or she look like? What will he or she be like? How will he or she treat me?* These are all normal questions to ponder when thinking about the prospect of your potential life partner. At the end of the day, if you're going to commit yourself to sharing your life, heart, mind, soul, body, and time with someone else forever, you definitely want to be attracted to that person. Likewise, I'm sure that you'll want to enter into such a partnership with someone who's going to treat you with love, honour, and respect. You want to be with a good person who's going to treat you well, and you want to be with the right person who's going to treat you right. I'm sure you've heard the saying, "Doing the right thing at the wrong time will bring about the wrong results." You may have heard a slightly different version, but either way, it's true.

It seems natural to think ahead and focus on the prospect of your future spouse, the person who will become your life partner. What you want and desire in your future spouse is a critical thing, and it's something that you should spend time thinking and praying about. But though this is good advice, it can become a distracting problem for you if you make it your main focus when preparing for marriage. This is because the most important factor when preparing for marriage is you – yes ... you!

Remember what I said in the opening of this introduction? Marriage has its own mathematics, and it creates its own sum; the end result is one unit in partnership. While preparing or thinking about marriage, it's important for you to understand that the quality of your "one" in your martial sum will result in the total and overall quality of your marriage. I'm saying that the quality of *you* will affect the overall quality of your marriage. In fact, the only thing that you have that will ensure your marriage will be a success is *you*. Too many times, we look to others to grant us quality without being quality people ourselves. If marriage is something that you desire, you need to focus on becoming and being a quality person who will be ready to enter into and build a quality marriage with a quality spouse.

Complete in Quality

Quality is simply the standard of one thing measured against another that is of the same or a similar kind. Quality is a degree of excellence – an amount, extent, or level to which something happens or is present in something. When questioning the quality of someone, you're basically questioning the general standard of excellence that resides within him or her. *Excellence* is the quality of being noticeably outstanding. All quality is measured and assessed by the degree of excellence within it. Quality can be measured, assessed, or summed up via percentages. In that regard, the highest degree of excellence 100 per cent.

Each and every person possesses a quality percentage. The percentage has nothing to do with being a perfect person; in fact, there is no such person. There is, however, the potential to become a complete person within all of us. We may not be perfect people, but we have the capacity to become completely wholesome people. Your degree of *completeness* results in the total quality of your individual self. Your percentage can range from 0 per cent to 100 per cent. And the level of your completeness as an individual will affect the quality of your marriage percentage as a whole.

Marriage has been ordained by God to be a lifelong partnership. When you look at the bigger picture, it's clear that marriage was designed to result in a mathematical sum of one wholly complete man and one wholly complete woman who come together to be one wholly complete unit.

Yes, you need to be with a quality person; and yes he or she needs to be complete. But your focus right now should be making sure that *you're* one hundred per cent whole for yourself and your future spouse. The questions you should be asking yourself when thinking about marriage include the following: *Am I whole? Am I 100 per cent complete?* You might be wondering, *What do you mean I should ask myself whether I'm whole? What does it mean to be 100 per cent complete? How am I supposed to become complete?* I'll answer your questions: to be complete for yourself is to be complete for your marriage, and marriage is a disposition. If marriage is a disposition, being complete within yourself must mean being complete within your own disposition. To broaden my answer: to be complete with yourself is to be whole within your heart, your soul, and your mind.

So the question now is, are you whole? Are you 100 per cent whole within your disposition? Are you 100 per cent within your heart, soul, and mind? To know whether you're truly whole within yourself, you first have to know what it is that causes us to be complete individuals. So what is it that makes us complete human beings?

Love and Wisdom

The way to become completely whole within yourself is to possess *love* and *wisdom*. A lot of times, we focus on love without focusing on wisdom, which doesn't make sense. Why? Because love is wisdom and wisdom is love. The two are synonymous; they cannot be separated because the two are the same. You can look at love and wisdom as being one whole unit in partnership. One does not work without the other; and without both being present, neither will function properly. If you're going to be whole within yourself and whole in your future marriage – if you're going to be a quality person in a quality relationship, if you're going to be a quality spouse who marries a quality spouse and has a quality marriage – you're going to have to become whole through love and through its wisdom.

Becoming whole in love and wisdom is a process. For some, the process will be straightforward and easy; for others, it might be difficult and painful (as it was for me). For me, the process was difficult because of my past and my disposition. My experiences in life created a fragmented disposition that needed healing, mending, cleaning, and resurrecting. I had to face the reality that I was a good person, but not a quality person. The process was uncomfortable, frustrating, distressing, and sometimes disturbing. Issues needed to be faced and addressed, some of which I didn't want to deal with. But not dealing with the issues of the past was hindering me from being a quality person for me and my future spouse. I'm glad to say that I stayed the course: in spite of all I went through in the process, I'm now 100 per cent complete. And it's all because I learned to understand love and receive its wisdom.

By reading this book, you're committing yourself to becoming a quality person. We're going to go through this process together. You might get sad, frustrated or angry when reading some parts of the book, but I want you to know that, no matter how you feel, I'll be here. No matter how you feel, though, keep reading the book. Why? Because you deserve to be healed, mended, cleansed, whole, and complete for you and your future spouse.

CHAPTER 1

Me, Myself, and I

You are unique, intricate, intriguing, and fascinating. All that makes you who you are is more complex than any hard drive on the face of the planet. There are so many components that come together to make you, but we can categorise these components into three major groups: *temperament, personality,* and *character* ... also known as *me, myself* and *I. Me, myself,* and *I* are the categories of your self-package: your *nature,* your *values,* and your *appearance.* Once you understand the components within these three categories, you'll be in a position to better know and understand who you are.

Often, when introducing or explaining yourself to others, you might try to sum up the totality of yourself through your personality. The word *personality* is the most common word in the three major categories that make up you. It's a word that has become famous, and one that has helped make people famous. For instance, reality TV stars are referred to as *personalities* or *famous personalities*.

Frequently, we say things confidently without really understanding what we are stating. This is true most of the time when we make statements about ourselves using the word *personality*. When trying to justify your actions to someone else or even yourself, you might say, "Well that's my personality." Alternatively, you might say, "This is my personality, who I am – love it or hate it, this is who I am." These statements (along with many others that include the word *personality*) are misused by many people when they refer to themselves. The word has become a cliché.

It's important for you to understand that your personality is an essential part of who you are as an individual and that it plays a major role in the overall package of you. Still, it's equally important for you to understand that your personality doesn't carry as much weight as you may think. In order to understand your personality, you're going to have to understand what your temperament is. Every structure has a base, and everything that has been constructed started off with a foundation. Your *me* is the base for your *myself* – in other words, your *temperament* is the foundation of your *personality*.

Me: My Temperament

Understanding the Meaning of Temperament

First, the word *temperament* is a psychological term that refers to certain aspects of an individual's personality. Temperaments are a way to classify people's emotional attitudes, which classify the foundations of our personalities. Temperaments are not specific or detailed, and they don't make up every detail of a person's personality. Temperaments are more categorical: *Cat* or *Dog*, for example. They are not as specific as words such as *Panther* or *Boston Terrier*. Personality and temperament are not synonymous. Your temperament is just one of the many facets that make up your overall personality.

The Four Fundamentals

The four temperaments is a proto-psychological theory that suggests that there are four fundamental personality types. These four fundamental personality types are as follows: *choleric* (ambitious and leader-like), *sanguine* (pleasure-seeking and sociable), *phlegmatic* (relaxed and thoughtful), and *melancholic* (analytical and literal). Most proponents of this theory suggested that the types could be mixed. Four is a very limiting number, though, and most people don't fit into just one of the four fundamental temperaments. These people are described in terms of temperament blends. Blends consist of primary and secondary temperaments. The primary temperament is the one that describes the most obvious part of an individual's personality, whereas the secondary temperament serves to flesh out the primary in more detail. An individual blend, for example, could be choleric–sanguine or melancholic–phlegmatic.

Temperaments Are not Mutually Exclusive

Temperaments should never be seen as part of a list; instead they should be seen as a whole. Temperaments are not determined by traits, but they can be described using traits. Temperaments are like dot-to-dot puzzles: you have to connect the dots to see the bigger picture when determining your temperament. You might find that you have traits from all of the fundamental temperaments, but only one or two of them fit you perfectly.

All stars are bright, but not everything that is bright is a star. Melancholics are sensitive, but being sensitive does not make you partially melancholic. There isn't really a melancholic trait; the melancholic temperament can be described using a list of traits, but a person is not partially melancholic just because he or she has one trait from that list. All humans have a wide variety of emotions, and it's the balancing of emotions, desires, and feelings that determine one's temperament. I'll explain what I mean. Let's use, for example, the choleric temperament. This temperament is more prone to anger than the other three (I know this first-hand!). Nevertheless, it's a fact that we all experience anger from time to time. Being angry or acting in an aggressive manner and being choleric are not synonymous. If you're angry or aggressive frequently, however, you may be choleric.

Temperaments Stay the Same by Nature and Do not Change by Nurture

Whether your temperament fits solely into one of the four fundamentals or whether it's a blend, one vital thing you need to understand is that your temperament won't change. Your temperament is innate, not learned. Your temperament is not a passing mood; it is the foundation of your emotional nature, which stays constant throughout your life despite personality changes.

As you mature physically, you may build muscle, put on weight, lose weight, grow hair, lose hair, get tattoos, wear jewellery, or wear coloured contact lenses. Still, you won't be able to change your ethnicity. All the changes you make on the surface won't change your origin. The same goes for your temperament. Your temperament is fundamental and irrevocable. Of course, your views, values, and confidence level change. In fact, it's your temperament that aids such changes.

It's not About What You Did, but How and Why You Did It

Your temperament can also be described as the *why factor*. It helps you learn why you choose to do specific things. Your temperament can also determine your approach to a specific situation or issue. Let's use the subject of abuse. If subjected to any abuse, a choleric person might become aggressive towards others as a means of venting and exerting dominance in the world. A phlegmatic person, though, may experience the same type of abuse and become self-destructive or catatonic. The same stimulus and the same experience will affect people in different ways due to each person's individual temperament.

Your temperament refers to the core aspects of your personality, such as whether you're introverted or extroverted. Knowing and understanding your temperament is critical because it will allow you to better understand yourself. Remember, your temperament is only one facet of your personality.

Myself, My Personality

The Difference between Temperament and Personality

Your personality is not inborn like your temperament; it's something that arises within you and advances as you mature. Your personality is a dynamic, organised set of characteristics that you possess (but did not learn), and it influences your emotions, thinking, motivations, and actions responses in various situations. Your personality also refers to the pattern of your thoughts, feelings, and behaviours (which strongly influences your attitude, expectations, self-perceptions, values, and beliefs). It also can be used to predict your reactions to other people, issues, and problems that you come across. Your personality traits can be positive or negative.

The Development of Personality

Your personality is a conglomeration of the decisions you have made throughout your life along with the memory of the experiences. Your temperament, though, is what contributes to the development of your personality.

The Mask

The word *personality* originates from the Latin word *persona*, which literally means *masks*. We typically think about masks as a means of disguising people's identities, but that was not the idea of the mask in the theatre of the ancient world. Rather, the mask was used as a way to represent the role of the character that the actor was portraying.

The You That We See

Your temperament, your experiences, and your environment all aided the development of the persona that you have today. Your persona is the quality that you portray or embody. The persona of your personality is the you that you show; it's the you that we see and perceive. Your personality typifies who you are; it's what represents you as an individual.

I, My Character

Character vs Personality

Your personality and character are both related to how you behave as an individual. Most of the time, *personality* and *character* are used interchangeably, but there is a very clear difference between one's personality and one's character. *Personality* is the image that one projects of oneself – how other people perceive one and how one deals with other people. *Character* can be described as a pattern of qualities that an individual has that is distinct from other humans' pattern of qualities. In short, personality is subjective and character is objective.

"When you choose your friends, don't be short-changed by choosing personality over character."   —*W Somerset Maugham*

Maugham's words clearly indicate that there is a difference between character and personality. You may have an excellent character, known for being reliable and talented, but you may also be shy and socially awkward. On the other hand, you may be extremely nice and fun to be around, but also unreliable and sneaky.

Your personality is reflected in your outer appearance and behaviour, which may or may not reflect your inner character. Personality can be glorified with the use of various different masks and is often developed to make one's life easier. Personality can be thought of as the polishing of character – if one is portraying one's real identity, that is.

Character

Your character refers to your ethical and moral values. Your character is moulded, generally, by the kind of environment that you live in. Your character functions along with the help of your mind and your feelings. Character is often regarded as the *true self,* which means that it represents the deep-rooted attributes that you possess as an individual. You can't disguise your ethical or moral values like the persona of your personality.

Comparison between Character and Personality

Attributes:

Character: loyalty, honesty, trust, responsibility, respect, leadership, courage, and constancy.

Personality: social, friendly, funny, and passionate.

Defined by:

Character: who you are.
Personality: what you seem to be.

Focus:

Character: one's mental and moral qualities.
Personality: one's outstanding characteristics.

Components:

Character: distinctive, persistent, and strong characteristics.
Personality: consistent expressions that impact actions and behaviours.

Character: your soul; the real you.

Personality: your mask, your persona, and your appearance.

So there you have it: the house of yourself is a construction of your temperament, character, and personality. They all have various components and work together to create you.

CHAPTER 2

The Quality of Yourself

Your character is what defines who you truly are. You can look at it like this: your temperament is the base of the house of yourself; your personality is the decor of yourself, and your character is the house itself. All three of these elements coexist in the core of your soul, but your character is the chief element.

Your character's components can also be described as your quality components. It's important to know these components and understand how they function. I've listed nine of these key components in this chapter, and we will examine their functions.

1. Your Attitude

Your attitude can be defined as an expression of favour or disfavour, or as a positive or negative evaluation of people, events, activities, ideas, etc. Your attitudes are formed by your past and present. Your attitudes are measurable and changeable. Your attitude influences your emotions and behaviours.

2. Your Behaviour

Your behaviour is a range of actions and habitual gestures that stem from your systems or artificial entities in conjunction with your environment (both mental and physical). Your behaviour is the response of your system to various stimuli – whether external or internal, overt or covert, conscious or subconscious, voluntary or involuntary.

3. Your Emotions

The functioning of your emotions is closely linked to the arousal of your nervous system. Various states and strengths of arousal relate to particular emotions. Your emotions manifest themselves psychologically and physically. The psychological side of your emotions entails acquiring knowledge via your thoughts, experiences, and senses. On the physical side, your emotions are a complex state of feelings that results in your corporeal changes that influence behaviour.

4. Your Expectations

Your expectations are beliefs based upon the future. Expectations can be realistic or unrealistic. An advantageous expectation that is unrealistic almost always results in disappointment.

5. Your Self-Perception

Self-perception is the act of developing your own attitudes by observing your behaviour and drawing conclusions. Self-perception is supposed to be formed by carefully assessing the internal process of thinking and the states of your moods. However, this isn't usually how people determine their attitudes. Instead, they induce their attitudes and interpret their behaviours irrationally. It's in this same way that we tend to explain the behaviours of others.

6. Your Belief

Belief is the psychological state in which an individual holds an opinion, proposition, or conclusion to be true.

7. Your Values

Values come in different forms. A personal value can be absolute or relative. A principle value is a premise upon which other values and measures of integrity (the state of being whole, strong, and moral) are based. Values can be subjective or objective. Subjective values are based upon personal feelings like such as the desire to get married or stay single, or the desire to avoid pain. These types of values are influenced by one's personal feelings, opinions, and tastes. Objective values vary depending upon the individual and the culture, and they are aligned with beliefs or belief systems. These types of values include moral and ethical values, ideological values, social values, and aesthetic values.

Values can also be defined as broad preferences concerning appropriate courses of action or outcomes. Typically, values reflect an individual's sense of what is right and what is wrong, or what should or shouldn't be. For example, *equal rights for all; excellence deserves admiration; everyone deserves a second chance;* and *people should be treated with respect and dignity at all times* all represent possible values. Values tend to influence attitudes and behaviours. A value system is a set of consistent values and measures.

8. Your Social Adjustments

Social adjustment is a psychological process. It is the effort you make in order to cope with new values, standards, or needs in order to be accepted. In a nutshell, adjustment is the psychology of getting along with other members of society to the very best of your ability.

9. Your Motivation

Motivation is a state of mind, an inner driving force that compels an organism to act towards a desired wish or goal. It elicits, controls, and sustains certain goal-directed behaviours. When motivation is activated, it has physiological, cognitive, behavioural, and social affects. Motivation may be rooted in a basic impulse to optimise your well-being, minimise physical pain, or maximise pleasure. Motivation can also begin from specific physical needs, such as drinking, eating, sleeping, and sex. For example, thirst is a motivation that elicits the desire to drink; sex is the motivation for physical gratification.

The Quality of Your Components

These nine key components work individually and collectively to form your character. After looking into the function of these components, it should be clearer why your character is the defining element of the trinity of yourself (and why your quality is based within your character). The ways you perceive, think, and act make up your character.

If you really want to understand the real state of your character, you're going to have to look at the making of it. What I'm saying is, you're going to have to face the reality that has moulded you. Unlike your temperament, which is inborn, and your personality, which arises all by itself, your character is formed. In order to fully understand why you are the way you are, you need to face reality. After all, reality holds the answer to the quality level of your character.

The Reality of Yourself

Your life is a living reality. Reality is the state of a thing as it actually exists. Therefore, the current state of your existence is your reality. Your reality and your existence are lived externally and internally, outwardly and inwardly – and both are obvious and hidden by turns. As it stands, your reality has been built upon circumstances, actions, and facts that have caused something to happen in or around you.

Your past circumstances contributed to the current quality of your life. Your life's current quality condition is based upon what others have done to you and what you've seen done. The totality of who you are, along with what you've become as an individual person, is a direct result of the decisions that you've made following a life experience.

Your experiences in life are things that have left impressions on you. Your experiences are felt externally and internally. You become aware of things through observations. Everything that you have noticed has been registered in your mind; all that you've seen with your eyes has been experienced through your mind. Through your many life experiences, you've gained knowledge. Each and every experience you've had automatically taught you a lesson. Then through that life lesson your understanding of things were then based according to the particular teacher who taught you the lesson.

Life Taught You Everything

Life is amazing. When you take time to see it for what it really is, you realise that life is truly amazing. It's remarkable because it didn't appear to be what it was when we first started experiencing it. On the day of your birth, life outside of your mother's womb didn't announce itself formally as a classroom (even though that was exactly what you stepped into). Yes, on the day of your birth, you stepped into the biggest classroom in all creation. This classroom has taught you many lessons through an abundance of experiences and a multitude of teachers. Everything you've experienced, you've lived; everything you've lived, you learned; and everything you've learned, you've become. Your learning made you who you are.

Quality Produces Quality

As life was teaching you through your experiences, it was moulding your sense of normalcy. Every impression that was imbedded in you through your countless experiences moulded you. The decisions you made during or directly after your experiences are what formed your character. Your life experiences were developing your characteristics that would become your typical way of living life and responding to its experiences. Your normal responses were being created, and your regular was becoming your reality.

In all of this, your normal was becoming natural. The nature of your instincts was being established. Your instincts were being established along with your natural intuition – what you feel to be true even without conscious reasoning. Your self, your normal, and your natural are what you are, and your quality is what defines the quality of your reality.

CHAPTER 3

The Lesson Is
within the Imagery

A parable is a very simple story that is used to illustrate a moral or spiritual lesson. The basis of the story is concerned with the principles of right and wrong behaviour. As simplistic as a parable may be, it also holds within it the ability to convey a life-changing lesson.

Jesus loved illustrating life-changing lessons through the imagery in parables. There's one particular parable that He shared in the book of Mathew that I would like to discuss. This parable is enlightening, and it is very fitting for the theme of this book. *The New Living Translation* subtitled this parable with the following words: "Building on a Solid Foundation." *The New International*

Version subtitled it as follows: "The Wise and Foolish Builders."
The King James Version subtitled it as follows: "Build on the Rock."

"Therefore whoever hears these sayings of Mine, and does them, I will liken him to a wise man who built his house on the rock: and the rain descended, the floods came, and the winds blew and beat on that house; and it did not fall, for it was founded on the rock. But everyone who hears these sayings of Mine, and does not do them, will be like a foolish man who built his house on the sand: and the rain descended, the floods came, and the winds blew and beat on that house; and it fell. And great was its fall."
—*Matthew 7:24–27*

Illustrated Houses

With this story, Jesus chose to illustrate His message using the imagery of two men working on their separate housing projects. The emphasis in the lesson wasn't placed upon the construction of their houses; in fact, He placed no emphasis whatsoever on the actual work that went into making the houses. He deliberately emphasised the grounds upon which they chose to build their houses.

The structure of each man's house was referred to as *it*. *It* is not clear or specific. The word *it* in this parable is actually the Greek word εκεινοσ, and it can be defined as follows: he, she, them, those. Thus, the men were actually building their selves as if they were building houses. They were building their *persons*; they were building their *realities*; they were building their *lives*;

and they were building their *relationships*. Jesus purposefully illustrated the realities of these two men's lives and relationships as houses. Why?

Why a House? Why not a Journey?

Many people refer to life as a journey. They describe life as a road or a path that we travel along daily. I've almost always pictured life that way because that's how I learned about life. Nearly every preacher I encountered illustrated life via that metaphor during their sermons. But that is not how Jesus illustrated the reality of life to us through the parable in Matthew.

I'm not saying that life isn't like a journey because, in some respects, it is. But in this parable, Jesus causes us to ask the question, "Why a house and not a journey?" Why does Jesus metaphorically liken our lives, our realities, and our relationships to a house and not a walk down a long and bendy road? For us to better understand why He chose to liken us to houses, we first need to understand the purpose of a house.

Houses vary in shape, form, and size, but they all share a common purpose. A house is anything that inhabits a person or anything of value that needs to be kept well. For instance, horses are housed in stables, fish are housed in tanks, and cows are housed in barns. Cars are housed in garages, foods are housed in refrigerators, and cutlery is housed in kitchen drawers. Money is housed in banks, jewellery is housed in beautiful boxes, and gold bars are housed in metal vaults. To be housed is to be kept safe, undamaged, and whole. Anything that is valued is kept, and that which is kept is housed.

Through the illustration of this parable, Jesus wanted you to understand that you are very much like the very house that you live in. You see, your soul is the house of yourself. Your soul houses the foundation of yourself, the definition of yourself, and the persona of yourself. It houses your temperament, your character, and your personality. Your soul is the very thing that houses your true self. But the lesson in the parable focused not on one's life, but on the grounds of one's life. The emphasis is on the quality conditions of the grounds of one's soul. It points out that the quality of the grounds of one's soul affects the quality of one's "house of life."

The Core of Your Being

Your soul is your core being, the centre of your life. Your soul is the vital force that gives life, power, and energy to your body, and it presents itself via your breathing. You breathe through your lungs, but what isn't as obvious is the place from which each breath is centred. This place is your soul. Your soul differs from all other parts of your body because it cannot be dissolved by death like your brain and heart, for example. Your soul is the place within you that is concerned with the principles of right and wrong. Your soul is the essence of your life that has been ordained to secure eternal blessedness and allow you to reach the highest end with God's help. Your soul is your being; it's that which has been designed for everlasting life. In short, your soul is all that you are.

"And the Lord God formed man of the dust of the ground, and breathed into his nostrils the breath of life; and man became a living being."   —*Genesis 2:7*

The Construction Grounds of the Self

Your soul has two construction grounds upon which it stands: your mind and your heart. The quality conditions of your heart and mind produce the quality condition of your soul. All that you are is centred in your soul, but constructed through your heart and mind.

Your Heart and Mind

Your heart is the organ that is situated in the centre of your circulatory system – that is why it is regarded as the seat of life. Your heart denotes the centre of all of your spiritual and physical life. Your heart is where your feelings, emotions, and will come from. Understanding also resides in your heart.

You could call your mind your intellectual factory. Understanding and perception occur there, as well as thoughts, feelings, and opinions. Your mind receives and processes your thoughts, whether they are good or bad. Your mind is the breeding ground for your imagination (it's also your receiving ground for insight). Your mind houses reason and allows for the reception of spiritual truth and the perception of divine things. It also allows you to recognise what is good and what is evil. Your mind has the power to consider things calmly, soberly, and impartially (or irrationally).

The Two Grounds Are Connected

Everything that runs around in your mind filters down to your heart; everything that consumes your mind flows to and through your heart; and everything that you think in your mind you manifest through your heart. The scripture says, "For as he thinks in his heart, so is he" Proverbs 23:7. In other words, as you ponder, your will is established. Why? Because your mind is the gatekeeper of your heart. Another proverb in the Bible explains this same truth in a different way: "Keep your heart with all diligence, for out of it spring the issues of life" Proverbs 4:23. If I were to paraphrase this scripture according to its original form in its original context, it would say something like this: watch over your heart in order to keep it from any form of danger, just like a prison guard stands watch over an inmate. The key word in the first half of this verse is *diligence*. Diligence is a mental function that takes place via your mental facilities. Your mind and heart are what your soul stands upon; this is why Jesus focused His attention on both grounds in the parable.

The men in this parable were essentially building their characters, their behaviours, their attitudes, and their realities. The one who built his life upon the sand didn't do very well. He lost his house to the waves of the storm of life. The other man managed to accomplish a great deal. Because he built his house on the rock, he was able to withstand every strong wave that the storms of life threw at him. His house, his life, his soul, his relationship, and his character were all able to remain intact because his foundation was excellent. His disposition was whole, right, and intact.

The grounds upon which you build your character will either be sandy or on a firm rock. Sand and rock were the only two options that Jesus gave in the illustration, so these are the only two options that you have to build your life, soul, character, reality, and relationships upon. So what we now have to determine is whether you're sandy or firm in your disposition.

CHAPTER 4

Quicksand-Minded and Sandy-Hearted

Whenever you find yourself at the beach or the seaside, you'll find yourself walking, sitting, or lying on sand. If you go there with children, you'll watch them as they play around, building castles and towers out of sand and decorating them with seashells. You might find the feeling of sand upon your skin to be comfortable or uncomfortable. Either way, if you go to the beach, you must trust the material of sand enough to support your body. As much as you might trust it, I'm sure that you don't really know what sand is or what it's composed of exactly. When I went to the beach when I was younger, I didn't really know what sand was – and honestly, I didn't really care to know. It was only after reading the parable in Matthew that I decided to find out what sand was.

The Substance of Sand

During my research, I found out that sand is a naturally occurring, granular material that is composed of finely divided rocks and mineral particles. The composition and quality of sand is highly variable depending upon numerous factors. So there you have it: sand is broken, tiny pieces of rock. There is nothing wholesome about sand because sand represents brokenness.

Quicksand

While researching sand, I found out that there is a type of sand called *quicksand*. Quicksand is a colloid hydrogel. A colloid is a substance microscopically dispersed throughout another substance (meaning that the substance is so small that it can be made visible only with a microscope). A hydrogel is a gel in which the liquid component is water. Quicksand is a colloid hydrogel consisting of sand, silt, clay, and saltwater.

Quicksand forms in saturated, loose sand (sand that is absorbed and thoroughly soaked in water) when the sand is agitated. It appears in areas with high water pressure, where the sand opens up for a minute, causing the water to saturate the sand. When the water in the sand cannot escape, it creates a liquefied soil that loses strength and becomes incapable of supporting any weight. Liquefaction is a special case in the world of quicksand. It occurs by way of pressure or shock. An earthquake immediately increases the pressure of shallow groundwater in quicksand. The saturated, liquefied soil loses strength, causing buildings and other objects on the surface to sink down or fall over. With quicksand, the saturated sediment (which is the matter that settles to the bottom of a liquid) may appear quite solid, but a sudden change in pressure or a shock can initiate liquefaction. It is the cushioning of water that gives quicksand and other liquefied sediments their spongy, fluid-like texture. After liquefaction occurs, any objects in liquefied sand sink to the level at which the weight of the object is equal to the weight of the displaced soil and water mix (the submerged object floats due to its buoyancy). Try to remember this information because we're going to come back to this idea soon. But for now, I want to introduce you to the word *geology*.

Geology is the science that examines the physical structure and substance of the Earth – its history, the rocks that it is made of, and the processes by which they change. Geology can also refer generally to the study of the solid features of any celestial body (such as the geology of a moon or Mars). The individual geology of the two men in the parable of the wise and foolish builder was the main focus point of the lesson. To better understand this point, I want to discuss briefly the geology of soil. The geology of soil is a very broad subject, so I'll just review with you the three main categories of soil. Please don't switch off because this is all going to make sense very shortly – and it will help a great deal!

Topsoil, Subsoil, and Substratum

Topsoil is the surface, the outermost layer of soil. It may be only an inch or so deep on thin, mountainous land. It usually ranges between a couple of inches and a few. Topsoil has the highest concentration of organic matter, and it is where most of the Earth's biological soil activity occurs. Because of its organic richness, it's generally a lot easier to handle than subsoil. Topsoil cultivates better than the layer of soil that is beneath it, and it's a lot less sticky than subsoil. Despite these advantages, it does have some disadvantages, including the sustenance of weeds.

Subsoil is the layer of soil under the topsoil. Like topsoil, subsoil is composed of a variable mixture of small particles, such as sand, silt, and clay. It lacks the organic matter and humus content of topsoil. Subsoil is usually lighter in colour than topsoil; it's very sticky, less fertile, and more difficult to handle. However, subsoil is generally fairly easy to improve. The third layer (beneath the subsoil) is the substratum. This is the underlying layer or substance, which can be residual bedrock, sediment, or aeolian deposits.

You might be wondering why I felt it necessary to share all of that knowledge with you. What has the geology of soil got to do with the parable in regards to the sand or the rock? Those are good questions. Fortunately, I have equally good answers for you. Jesus was focusing on the grounds and their quality. As mentioned earlier, your heart and your mind are the construction grounds for the development of your soul. Just as the geology of soil has three core layers, so does the grounds of your mind. In fact, the geology of soil is extremely similar to the grounds of your mind. Your mind, as a whole, is made up of three layers: your conscious mind, your preconscious mind, and your unconscious mind.

Your Conscious Mind

Your consciousness is the current mental state that you're in. It makes you aware of your external surroundings or things within yourself. Your consciousness is the chief executive control system of your mind. It is what gives you the ability to perceive, to sense, and to feel. It is the most alert and wakeful place in your mind. It's also the place where your sense of selfhood is conjured.

Your Preconscious Mind

Preconsciousness is a state of mind in which your thoughts are unconscious. This mindset handles matters that are not yet relevant to you, matters that are hidden but not repressed (and therefore available to be pushed into one's conscious mind). Just so we're clear, I'll give you an example of how your preconscious state of mind works. Here, all your thoughts are being remembered, such as your cell phone number or child's birthday. When you need to consciously recover this information, you dip into the hidden place of your preconscious mind and bring them into your conscious mind.

Your Unconscious Mind

Your unconscious mind processes information automatically, including perception, memory, language, and motivation. During this process, your unconscious mind is not available to introspection. Thus, even though your unconscious mind is processing things, you're unaware of that process and unable to examine or observe those things. Your unconscious mind has a will and a purpose of its own that cannot be known by your conscious. Your unconscious mind exists well under the surface of your conscious awareness, and it can be viewed as the repository of your mind – a place where things may be stored.

Considerable empirical evidence suggests that the unconscious mind contains repressed feelings, traumatic memories, painful emotions, subliminal perceptions, thoughts, habits, automatic skills, and automatic reactions (it may also contain hidden phobias and desires).

The degree to which your unconscious mind influences your decision-making is a topic that has been debated by neuroscientists and psychologists around the world for quite some time. Still, the fact that it plays a role in cognitive activity is undeniable. Your unconscious mind – whether you're aware of it or not – can impact your behaviour.

A Sandy Psyche

What's important for you to understand in all of this is that every broken experience produces a sandy experience, and these sandy experiences produce sandy memories. The sandy memories, in turn, produce sandy preconscious and unconscious states of mind. All of the different sandy thoughts, memories, and experiences that are hidden and embedded in the layers of your preconscious and unconscious mind (when recalled to your conscious mind) automatically affect your heart. In essence, all of the brokenness of a sandy psyche establishes a sandy disposition, which ultimately produces a sandy person with a sandy character.

CHAPTER 5

Are You Insane?

The Symptoms of a Sandy Psyche

Craziness is a symptomatic manifestation of a sandy psyche. I once heard author and pastor, Dr Mike Murdock say in a meeting, "Not all of the insane are in the asylum." The majority of the attendees burst into laughter, including me. The way in which he said it made us all laugh, but what he was saying was very true. Not all of the crazy people are in the asylum, but why? Because there are levels of craziness. People in the asylum require medical care. After all, they might hurt themselves or others around them. The asylum is a place of protection for those with a certain level of insanity.

Operating at any craziness level means that you're functioning in a foolish way. When Dr Mike Murdock said that not all of the insane are in the asylum, he was saying that not all of the foolish people were being treated for their foolishness. In other words, the foolish are walking among us. Foolishness entails acting in an unwise manner, lacking good sense, or lacking judgement. Acting foolishly prohibits you from being able to make good decisions.

Insane without a Clue

Have you ever seen an intelligent person do something stupid? It's not that the person is stupid, but the act is. In other words, it is a foolish act. I was one of those people at one time. I was one of the people that Dr Mike Murdock was talking about. I didn't know it at the time, but I was insane and acting foolishly in terms of my relationships. I was a shouter, screamer, thrower, puncher, etc. When I was mad, the other person knew it – it was obvious. I was almost always loud, and I could get physical, too. That's what I did with every man I dated. It was what I learned to do, so it's what I always did. If I wasn't shouting, screaming, or storming out of the flat, I would completely ignore my boyfriend. I could go a week without talking to him or responding to his texts. If he came around, I would pretend that he wasn't even there. At the time that I was doing all of this, I felt I was doing the right thing. I was just expressing my annoyance with him. Yes, I honestly felt like my actions were right. Nobody could tell me anything, not even my mum or my friends. But the truth of the matter was that I was completely wrong. I wasn't wrong because I wasn't wronged by him; rather, I was wrong because I responded inappropriately. Every time I did something crazy, I was unknowingly throwing sand at him. And each and every time that I was throwing sand at him, I was throwing sand at our relationship. Yep, here we go with that sand again. I should tell you now that another word for *foolishness* is *sand*.

You may have encountered sandy experiences that produced sandy dispositions, sandy preconsciousnesses, quicksand unconsciousnesses. And the end result may have been a sandy heart that manifested sandy actions. In essence, the sand in you caused you to act in a crazy way. You might have exhibited extreme anger or acted irrationally. If you act foolish in any way shape, or form, you're acting crazy. You might do things in your relationships that seem to be right and normal, but are actually foolish. I'll explain what I mean with a few examples of what seems to be normal in many relationships today. It's crazy to beat your girlfriend, even if that's what you saw your father do to your mother; it's crazy to cuss out your boyfriend even if that's how other couples in your neighbourhood carry on. It's madness to ignore the calls, texts, and e-mails of your partner for a whole week; it's madness to completely ignore your partner when in a social situation just to prove to others that you're extremely mad. It's insanity to post the argument you had with your partner on Facebook; it's insanity to slash the tyres of your partner's car just because he or she couldn't see you one night. In doing these sorts of things, you're throwing sand at your partner and producing a sandy relationship.

A lot of the time, we act out in a crazy manner and then try to justify our foolish behaviour by saying stuff such as the following: "She was rude to me first," "He did this," "She did that," "She disrespected me," or "He hurt my feelings." Of course, you might be telling the truth – he or she might have been wrong or acted poorly. But your response still can't be justified. Foolishness is foolishness ... end of story. Responding to people's foolishness with foolishness is just more foolishness.

Sand Produces Sandcastles

A broken psyche produces a messy relationship, and a messy relationship will always be wiped away by the storms of life. Remember the liquefaction process that I talked about in the previous chapter? The triggering of any brokenness in the unconscious layer of your mind is just like the liquefaction process of quicksand. Everything can seem fine and stable, but if a sensitive issue arises, everything can collapse. According to your individual temperament, the triggering of the liquefaction process of your unconscious mind will cause you to lose your temper or retreat. Without any warning, you change. When the liquefaction of your unconscious mind takes place, you act crazy and foolish.

If we take a moment to look back at the parable of the two builders, it's clear that the storm didn't cause the house to collapse; rather, the foolish behaviour caused the house to collapse. The foolishness of the man's psyche could not withstand the pressure of the storm because the foolishness of his actions carried no weight, no strength. His messy house was wiped out by the waters of the storms of life. When I look at the bigger picture, I believe that the house the man built was a sandcastle. I believe this because he acted foolishly by building his house upon the sand. This means that he built his house *with* the sand. He was building his self and a relationship, but all he had to build with was what he was: sand. His mind was sandy, his heart was sandy, and his soul was sandy. Every time he went to build himself or his relationship, he built with sand. He built a sandy house upon sandy ground, and the waters wiped him away. He built a sandy character upon a sandy soul, which was constructed upon a sandy mind and heart, and the issue of life came along and reduced him to nothing. Sandy souls never stand for long.

You might be sandy due to the sand that was thrown at you (the things that you've seen or gone through in life). A sandy life experience can create a sandy mind, and a sandy mind, when triggered, produces sandy behaviour. You might even be sandy due to the misconceptions that you had about love and relationships. Your opinion regarding what true love and real relationships are might be totally messed up due to the messy and sandy views of others who influenced you. What you saw, read, or heard might be based upon faulty logic.

God doesn't want you to be sandy. He never created you to be in such a condition, but the fact of the matter is, you can become sandy. Fortunately, you can change. The quicksand of your unconscious mind and the sand that is lying dormant in your preconscious mind (along with the sand in your heart) can

CHAPTER 6

Re-Establishing Yourself with Wisdom

"'For I know the thoughts that I think toward you,' says the Lord, 'thoughts of peace and not of evil, to give you a future and a hope.'" —*Jeremiah 29:11*

The Concept of Establishment

God conceived you in His mind, spoke you into existence. He thought you into purpose, spoke you into purpose so that His divine purpose for you could be established. God establishes things. Everything He says or does is to establish something. To establish something is to raise it up, strengthen it, or cause it to succeed. When something is established, it is set, fulfilled, and accomplished. An establishment is a foundation, but not all foundations are establishments. The difference between an establishment and any other foundation is that an establishment is *built,* and all other foundations are just laid. An establishment is *secure,* but not all foundations have security within them. God wants us to build great lives with great relationships upon a heart, a mind, and a soul that is established in His love and through His wisdom.

There's More to This Foolishness Than We Think

God has made every provision for you to be established, and this provision starts with your choice. Yes, becoming established within your disposition is a choice – a choice to favour wisdom over foolishness. Nobody wants to be foolish; the word *foolish* has no good connotations attached to it whatsoever. Actually, the word for *foolish* in the scripture of the two builders is the Greek word μοροσ, and that word translates to *being godless.* Words derived from this word include dull, stupid, and heedless.

Unfortunately, if you haven't been open to God, you've been foolish. If you've been building your reality without being totally open to God, you've been foolish. Even if you've been trying to build your life and your relationships to last, you've been attempting to do the right thing in the wrong way. You were attempting to build your life and your relationships upon the unbuilt and unestablished; you were trying to build externally without building internally; you were attempting to build above the surface without building below the surface. When you take a minute to look at how you've been attempting to build your life and your relationships, you might be able to see that results aren't great. Basically, you've shut out the ideas that God has for you, which exist within His wisdom. I can put my hand up and admit that I've been totally foolish in my life. I was foolish because I wasn't living my life and building my reality with the wisdom of God. I was heedless – I wanted to do my own thing my own way, so I blocked out the wisdom of God. I felt that I was more than capable of handling my own life in my own way. In a nutshell, I was stubborn.

In the parable of the two builders, the man who successfully established his house on the rock was able to do so because he was wise. He acquired wisdom and utilised it to build his disposition and his relationships. Wisdom was the most essential component in establishing his firm foundation. When I was attempting to lead my life in my own way, I believed that I was doing so with wisdom. I really couldn't understand why my reality was crumbling, why it wasn't standing up like the wise builder in the parable. I eventually came to realise that I was applying wisdom in the building of my reality, but I was using a guarantee-to-fail "wisdom." There are only two types of wisdom in the world (see James 3:13–18). The first type of wisdom is authentic and leads to success; it is the wisdom of God. The second type is the one that I was using: the wisdom of man. Many people use human wisdom. This clearly doesn't work. And when that wisdom fails you, you must seek the wisdom of God.

So What Is the Wisdom of God?

Wisdom, in essence is, skill. The wisdom of God is the skill of God. Skill is having the ability to do something well in a good or appropriate way given the facts or circumstances.

How Is the Skill of God Formed?

The skill of God consists of two things: knowledge and understanding. Knowledge is awareness, perception, information, and intelligence. Understanding is the ability to reason, consider, feel, and discern. In simple terms, knowledge is the *know,* and understanding is the *know how to.* Together, they produce skill, which is wisdom.

"For the Lord gives wisdom; from His mouth come knowledge and understanding."   —*Proverbs 2:6*

How Do I Get the Wisdom?

You get the skill and the wisdom of God, directly from the mouth of God: "For the Lord gives wisdom; from His mouth come knowledge and understanding" (Proverbs 2:6). You get the wisdom of God through the mouth of God. You receive the wisdom through His written word; the Bible, and from the words that He speaks directly to your heart and spirit.

"But He answered and said, 'It is written, "Man shall not live by bread alone, but by every word that proceeds from the mouth of God."   —*Matthew 4:4*

How Will I Know If I Have the Wisdom of God?

You'll know when you have the wisdom of God when you first receive a reverence for Him, when you start regarding Him and treating Him with the deepest respect. This is the first step to walking and living in the wisdom of God. This is how it's put in the book of Proverbs: "The fear of the Lord is the beginning of wisdom, and the knowledge of the Holy One is understanding" (Proverbs 9:10). "The fear of the Lord is the instruction of wisdom, and before honor is humility" (Proverbs 15:33).

Why Should I Get the Wisdom?

According to the wisest man who ever lived, wisdom is the most important thing. This means that wisdom should be first in place, time, order, and rank. Wisdom is the first of things, the beginning of things, the chief of things, and the best of things. "Wisdom is the principal thing; therefore get wisdom. And in all your getting, get understanding" (Proverbs 4:7).

The Wisdom of God Wants to Prove Itself to You

Proverbs Chapter 8 is subtitled differently (though only slightly) through the various translations of the bible. In the *New King James Version* (*NKJV*), it's subtitled, "The Excellence of Wisdom."

In the *New International Version* (*NIV*), it's subtitled, "Wisdom's Call." In the *New Living Translation* (*NLT*), it's subtitled, "Wisdom Calls for a Hearing," and in *The Message* (*MSG*), it's subtitled, "Lady Wisdom Calls Out."

Wisdom has a lot to say; it can really talk! It talks in the third person. Its style of talking is straight with no corners. Wisdom is not shy when talking; rather, it's extremely bold and confident while commanding your full attention. It has every right to act in this way because it has a tremendous résumé. It's excellent because of what it's done and accomplished in the past, and most importantly because of the entity with whom it worked first. Wisdom's first possessor was God, and its first job was making the Earth.

"The Lord possessed me at the beginning of His way,
Before His works of old.
I have been established from everlasting,
From the beginning, before there was ever an earth."
—*Proverbs 8:22–23*

Proverbs 8:22–23 allows us to understand that wisdom was the first thing that God created. Before He started making any plans for the earth, God attained wisdom. Before there was anything (even light), there was wisdom. God, first and foremost, made wisdom before carrying out any other work.

"When there were no depths I was brought forth,
When there were no fountains abounding with water.
Before the mountains were settled,

Before the hills, I was brought forth;
While as yet He had not made the earth or the fields,
Or the primal dust of the world.
When He prepared the heavens, I was there,
When He drew a circle on the face of the deep,
When He established the clouds above,
When He strengthened the fountains of the deep,
When He assigned to the sea its limit,
So that the waters would not transgress His command,
When He marked out the foundations of the earth,
Then I was beside Him as a master craftsman;
And I was daily His delight,
Rejoicing always before Him,
Rejoicing in His inhabited world,
And my delight was with the sons of men."
—*Proverbs 8:24–31*

The whole time that God was forming the earth and the sons of men, wisdom was with God, working beside Him. Wisdom was beside God on purpose, for a purpose. The reason wisdom was beside God from the beginning of time was because of its craftsmanship. Yes, wisdom was created by God to be beside God because wisdom is "a master craftsman."

Wisdom, the Master Craftsman

Wisdom is a master craftsman, a master workman, a supreme architect. Let's break this down. A master is one who has complete control over something; he or she possesses the ability to be the leader of a situation or a person. A workman is one who is employed to do manual labour. A craftsman is one who has specified skills in crafting. A crafter is skilful at making things with his or her hands. An architect is a person who designs buildings. He or she pays attention to each and every detail – drawing up the plans of a structure that needs to be erected. The plans of an architect are produced to show the look and functioning of a building. The job of an architect isn't just to produce plans, but also to supervise construction. Architects oversee the work that goes into the finalisation of the project.

In seeing all the attributes and qualities that wisdom possesses, we can understand why God possessed it first before starting any other work. Wisdom has all knowledge, all understanding, all skill, and all ability within its hands. The wisdom of God took the dust of nothing and created the most beautiful things in existence, such as the solar system, the mountains and rivers of earth, and human beings. Wisdom made all things beautiful and wonderful out of the dust of nothing, and God's wisdom will take the mess of your sandy psyche and transform you into a beautiful, complete person. The wisdom of God will never fail because that's not possible. It didn't fail God when it drew up its plans for the earth and all creation, so it won't fail you either. Via wisdom, the heavens and the earth were made, and via wisdom, your house can be rebuilt and re-established, too.

"Through wisdom a house is built, and by understanding it is established." —Proverbs 24:3

Wisdom is excellent. Her résumé is perfect, her history is everlasting. If you truly desire to rebuild your house, your life, your soul, and your character correctly, you must possess the excellence of wisdom. Wisdom has a certain way of working. It works to bring about harmony and order. It works with instructions, it has rules, and it has a set of commands. As excellent as wisdom is, its ways can feel somewhat uncomfortable at times, and its instructions can be somewhat hard to carry out. At the end of it all, though, its ways are always excellent.

CHAPTER 7

Out with the Old, in with the New

It's Time to Renovate Your Mind

In order for you to remove all the sand and quicksand from your psyche and your disposition, you must apply the wisdom of God that is in Romans 12:2.

"And do not be conformed to this world, but be transformed by the renewing of your mind, that you may prove what is that good and acceptable and perfect will of God."   —*Romans 12:2*

This scripture has within it an instruction and a process. The instruction is: "And do not be conformed to this world, but be transformed." The key word is *conformed.* To be conformed is to be fashioned alike. You can cut your mind and your character into a certain pattern or design, just as a tailor or a seamstress would do when making clothes. In essence, the wisdom in this instruction is to avoid the problems of this world. Many have already been conformed in their dispositions by the broken experiences that they've had in life. Many already have a sandy nature. This might seem hopeless, but the good news is that there's a *but:* "But be transformed by the renewing of your mind, that you may prove what is that good and acceptable and perfect will of God."

The first part of this process entails understanding that you need to be transformed, metamorphosed. You must undergo a process that will bring about a complete change in order to remove any sand or quicksand within you. You must renew your mind, renovate it. Going forth with the renewal process of your mind is just like renovating the house you live in: changing everything that makes the house and its inhabitants better off. The wisdom of God wants you to redo and redecorate your mind. He wants you to get rid of the old and bring in the new. He wants you to purge out the mess and bring in the fresh. He wants you to deal with the past and start afresh with the future. God wants you to renovate your mind; He wants you to dig and forgive.

Forgiveness

Forgiveness means different things to different people. At the end of the day, forgiveness is the act of letting something go. The *something* can be a situation, circumstance, experience, person, or group of people. Whatever the something is, forgiveness is designed to separate you from it.

Forgiveness is a process and its action is twofold. The first half of the process is acknowledgement, and the second half is digging and disposing. The first stage of the acknowledgement process is accepting that something is wrong or out of order. It is the act of recognising that something needs to be dealt with. It's all about looking at your current reality and looking back at what caused you to become sandy. In looking back, you might find that your sand was created by an interaction with a certain person. Your sand may stem from the environment that you were born into or grew up in. Your sand or quicksand may be a result of many things.

Offended, Insulted, and Disregarded

One of the first words that pops in your mind when you think about having to apply forgiveness may be *offence*. An offence is an annoyance or resentment brought about by a perceived insult. Over the course of your life, you've definitely been insulted and disregarded in some way by somebody else. People can be insulted physically, mentally, and emotionally. The issue with insults is that they make you feel worthless in some manner. Being disregarded is a horrible thing. It comes about when people don't pay attention to you.

In short, you've been offended, insulted, and disregarded in one way or another – even by people who allegedly love you. It might have been a parent, family member, friend, or ex-lover. It might have been someone you looked up to, respected, and admired. It might have been a complete stranger. Either way, you were, offended, insulted, and disregarded all the same.

Why We Don't Want to Forgive Them

Offences of any kind can be extremely painful and detrimental. As humans, we have a tendency to deal with offences in a certain way. If the offence was extremely painful, we may want to reverse the hands of time and erase the offences of the past. We know that we can't do this, of course. Still, we hold on to our offences as if they can be changed. If we're not hoping to travel back in time, we're hoping to be compensated for the offences via an apology or some commensurate action. At the end of it all, we want them to feel some sense of guilt about what they did. These feelings are normal, human nature.

Why We Hold onto the Sand

The way we react to offences may be different, but there are similarities. We either advertise our offences or hide them. By advertising our offences, we make it clear that we have been wronged. We make our offences known to all and sundry. We draw attention to our past and focus on a certain period of time. These are what I call *surface offences* – offences that are made known to all in order to defend ourselves.

We intentionally or unintentionally advertise our offences (discreetly or blatantly) in order to defend ourselves from getting hurt in the future. Nobody wants to get hurt; nobody wants to feel pain. Again, this is human nature.

If we're not advertising the offences, we're hiding them. We keep them within our minds, hearts, and souls. Harbouring offences is a very dangerous thing. Offences reside within us in many different forms. A lot of the time, it's not so much that you're holding on tightly to the offence, but rather, you're choosing not to deal with it. Instead, you tell yourself that it's okay when it obviously isn't. You tell yourself that the offence didn't matter without dealing with it. It is this way of dealing with our offences that causes the quicksand effect in your unconscious mind to occur. These are the hidden offences that cause our relationships to sink. Whatever it is, it must be recognised and accepted. You must accept that it was wrong and painful (and that it happened). Otherwise, you'll become afflicted with anger, frustration, fear, insecurity, sadness, confusion, or something else terrible. Once you've accepted the hurt, you can go on to the second and final stage of forgiveness: disposal.

We dispose of things every day by throwing them in the trash. Disposing of material things is not hard – you just pick it up and throw it away. When it comes to disposal in the realm of forgiveness, though, throwing things away isn't so easy. In fact, it can be terribly hard. Also, forgiveness can never be forced upon you; it is a choice that only you can make for yourself.

I Had to Dig It out and Toss It Up

I've been offended many times in my life by many different people. I've been insulted, disregarded, hurt, and wronged. I've held on tightly to some of my offences, and I've advertised some of them, too. At times, I felt that forgiveness would entail disrespecting myself. I felt as if forgiving others would add insult to injury. I felt as if forgiving them would be like saying that what they did wasn't wrong. I couldn't move forward. Even though I was a Christian and an ordained minister, I didn't feel that it was right to forgive them.

Still, I felt the need to deal with the offences that I carried. I felt like I had to deal with my surface offences and my hidden offences. I had to acknowledge that I had been wronged and address that hurt. Honestly, it was very uncomfortable, but amid the discomfort, I understood that it was necessary. As I was facing these offences, I started feeling things that I did not want to feel. The very feelings I was trying to avoid were manifesting in my heart, and the very thoughts I was trying to avoid were flooding my mind. I didn't like it. But amid the unwanted feelings and thoughts, I started to say out loud, "I don't want this ... It hurts. I don't want it anymore." I started weeping and saying, "Lord, help. Lord, help me let it go, release these feelings." You see, I had to feel it in order to acknowledge it. I had to dig it up and handle it by crying out to God. The feeling was horrible, and I did not want to harbour it, advertise it, or feel it; I just wanted to release it. So with my mind, my heart, and my words, I tossed it up to Him. I completely disposed of it by saying, "Painful experience, I don't want you anymore. I yield you to God. Yes, I'm tossing you up to Him today. I'm totally done with you. Goodbye." I had to call on God's grace to help me release it, and His grace came through for me. I turned to God and put my human logic aside; I entrusted God completely with the hurts and offences of my past. I came to the understanding that I couldn't love anyone the way they deserved to be loved while holding onto the pain caused by others.

As long as you hold onto the brokenness of your past experiences, brokenness will manifest itself in you. The sand of your past, as long as it is within you, will continue to make you crazy. Hurt manifests hurts. The offences you hold onto cause you to offend others. All that is within you is all that you're able to give. Your brokenness will continue to break those around you.

Out with the Old and In with the New

I want you to understand that God's grace will help you do what is right, even when it's hard for you to do it. You might have to forgive people who are dead, incarcerated, or living in another country. You might have to forgive people you haven't seen in years or people you see daily. You might not even care about the person, just the offence. Whether you're holding on tightly to your offence or kicking it under the carpet, the truth of the matter is that you are not dealing with the offence properly, and in doing so, you're causing harm to yourself and those around you. Whether the offences are surface offences or hidden ones, you need to deal with them. Whether you have to forgive others or yourself, call on God's grace to help you do so. If you chose not to deal with your offences, you will never be able to stand on the rock because the broken pieces of your sandy offences will stand in your way. Sand doesn't fly away; quicksand doesn't fly away. The sand and quicksand in your life will only be removed when you acknowledge it, dig it out, and toss it up. Digging can be a messy situation, but at the end of the day, once the sand and quicksand is removed, you'll be better off. Your space will be clear, and you'll be able to begin replacing the old with the new and renovating your mind successfully.

Wisdom wants you to get rid of all your offences and your misconceptions about love and relationships. (Don't forget about those misconceptions that we spoke about in Chapter 7 of this book.) You also have to be willing to let go and separate yourself from every false view that you've adopted over the years. You have to clear your mind of everything that you think you know, and you need to be open to the true view and understanding of love and relationships via the wisdom of God's love.

CHAPTER 8

Establishing a Concrete Soul

Erecting the Foundation

Just as a building is only as strong as what stands beneath it, so is a man only as strong as his soul. *Foundation* is the term typically used to describe the base of a building. The right term to describe the base of a strong building is *substruction*. Each strong building has more than an ordinarily laid foundation; it also has a building built under it that supports it and carries its weight. This means that a strong foundation is erected before the "surface" building is built on top of it. When the foundation itself is built in this way, the term *establishment* is applied to it.

When Jesus was describing the foundation of the wise man, He described it as a rock. When we look at the word *rock* in its original form, we understand that Jesus was saying that the disposition of the man had become as firm as a rock by renovating his mind. The man himself was likened to a rock because his soul had hardened. The wise man rebuilt his mind, soul, and disposition before he focused on building any relationships with anyone else. He established himself as a substruction, a foundation that could carry the weight of the responsibilities, pressures, and issues of life. He wanted the reality of his existence to be strong, so he chose to re-establish his soul before looking for love with a woman.

The Rock of Concrete

Our modern-day houses and their foundations are built with concrete. Concrete is a composite material (which means that it's formed by individual materials that form a larger structure that is better than the individual components). It is composed of aggregate (a coarse, granular material), which is embedded in a hard matrix of material, cement, which fills the space within the aggregate particles and glues them together to form a strong building material. The coarse aggregate materials in concrete include sand, gravel, and crushed stone or slag.

We are fleshly, earthen vessels formed from the very dust of the earth. As long as we are living and breathing on this earth, we are aggregate materials. Cement is a binder. It is a substance formed to set, harden independently, and bind other materials together as one substance. The strength and firmness in concrete comes from the strength that is embedded in the substance of cement. In order to create the concrete substance for the foundation of your soul, you're going to have to mix the aggregate of your being with the mixture of "cement."

The Cement of Love

Agape is one of the elements of love. It's the type of love that desires the highest good for the recipient. This type of love seeks to welcome, entertain, and please. Agape love desires nothing but the best for us in every area of our lives. Agape is not an emotion-based type of love; it is the type of love that loves you at all times. Agape love is *whole*, agape love is *full*, agape love is *complete*, agape love is *weighty*, and agape love is *secure*. Agape love is the cement and the binder that you need to mix with your soul in order to form the perfect substance to erect your strong, stable, and reliable foundation.

When your soul is mixed with the cement of agape, you feel complete. God wants your soul – your inner self, your disposition – to be so firmly and deeply fixed in the mass mixture of agape love to where you are fully strengthened. It makes your soul as secure and strong as a rock. It is agape that causes your soul to become a rock. It is agape that causes your realities and relationships to be founded and established correctly. It is agape that causes you to stand strong amid any and every storm.

Under the surface of his reality, the wise man's soul was as strong as a concrete, rock house. His soul was built, his soul was strong, his soul was steady, and his soul was unbreakable – all because he invested in his internal substruction. Anything and everything that needs to be built comes with a plan and some instructions. This is where listening to the wisdom of God came into play: the wise man heard God's instructions. He attended to His wisdom, and he carried out what the wisdom of God directed him to do. In doing so, his soul was established, like a rock.

If you are going to be like the wise man, you're going to have to follow the wise instructions of the Lord. But where do you start? What instructions should you follow first in order to begin building your substruction? The answers to all of these questions are pretty simple and can be found in Matthew:

"'Teacher, which is the great commandment in the law?' Jesus said to him, 'You shall love the Lord your God with all your heart, with all your soul, and with all your mind.' This is the first and great commandment. And the second is like it: 'You shall love your neighbor as yourself.' On these two commandments hang all the Law and the Prophets." —*Matthew 22:36–40*

Love Is Established only in Order

That passage allows us to understand that love has an order. The mixing and layering of the cement of agape must be done in a certain order. The foundation plans of love have an order; the re-establishing of authentic love has an order. In order to build the substruction correctly, you're going to have to follow its functioning instructional order. Many of us are trying to establish love, but we are unsuccessful at it because we aren't doing it properly. I know because I was one of those people. I was out of order with love.

"Do I Love You, God?"

The Matthew passage in discussion is one that I've been familiar with for a long time. I even know it by heart. At first, I thought I was applying it to my life properly. I loved God and tried my best to love my neighbours, so I believed I was doing well. One day, though, while reading my Bible during a time of devotion, I saw the scripture differently. While I was reading it, I felt that, even though I knew it, I didn't understand it. I was reading the scripture with a heavy, humble, and open heart that day, and I felt like my humility and my desire to see a real and better change in my life and in my relationships (even those with family members and friends) were allowing me to see beyond what I knew.

At that time, I began to question myself. I started asking myself questions like, *Do I really love God? How do I know whether I really love God? How do I even go about loving God?* I wasn't asking myself these questions in a state of guilt; I was asking myself these questions out of genuine curiosity. I wanted to make sure that I really loved God; I wanted to make sure that I was loving Him as He wanted me to: with all of my heart, soul, and mind.

A lot of the times, we know what to do without really knowing how to do it. At times, we can unintentionally deceive ourselves into believing that we know how to do something that we don't know how to do. When I questioned whether I really loved God,

I couldn't answer myself. I didn't know how to answer it. Not knowing how to answer my own questions let me know that I had to search within God's word to get the right answers. I looked up relevant scriptures, and this is what I found:

"If you love Me, keep My commandments."   *—John 14:15*

"A little while longer and the world will see Me no more, but you will see Me. Because I live, you will live also. At that day you will know that I am in My Father, and you in Me, and I in you. He who has My commandments and keeps them, it is he who loves Me. And he who loves Me will be loved by My Father, and I will love him and manifest Myself to him."   *—John 14:19–21*

So it's as simple as that? All we need to do to love God is keep His commandments? Honestly, I was expecting to find something deeper than that – I'm not sure why. To really grasp what Jesus was saying, I focused on the key word: *commandments*. When we look at the word *commandments* in John 14, we see that many words are derived from it: injunction, authoritative, prescription and precept. An *injunction* is an authoritative order or warning. When something is *authoritative*, it's in a position of reliability and trust. It is clear information, advice, or instruction. When something is authoritative, it's considered to be the best of its kind, which makes it unlikely to be improved upon. It proceeds out of an official source, and it requires compliance or obedience. A *prescription* is a written instruction. We receive prescriptions from our doctors when we're unwell, and these prescriptions authorise us to be issued medicines, remedies, or treatments that are prescribed to make us feel better. This, however, is not the type of prescription that is being indicated in John 14. The prescription here is a prescribed rule that is in accordance with how a thing should be done – like a precept. A *precept* is a general rule that is intended to regulate (control) behaviour or thought.

Thus, God's commandments are His authoritative, prescribed rules. They are what He wants us to do. They clearly show us the ways in which He wants us to go. His commandments deal with our hearts, minds, and souls. His commandments are in place to keep us, protect us, help us, and bless us. They are in place to produce good, not evil. They are in place to benefit us. Therefore, loving God is obeying all that He says.

First, Seek

Getting to the point of obeying God's commandments is a process. The first step is seeking Him. After all, you cannot obey that which you do not know, and you cannot use that which you don't have. The whole objective in seeking is to find. Therefore, if we want to love God by obeying what He decrees, we're going to have to *want to know* what God is saying first. There are different ways we can seek God.

1. Seeking God in and through His Word

"Ask, and it will be given to you; seek, and you will find; knock, and it will be opened to you. For everyone who asks receives, and he who seeks finds, and to him who knocks it will be opened."

—*Matthew 7:7–8*

The Bible consists of 66 books with 1,189 chapters. There are new and old testaments. The Bible is full of stories, characters, and people's life experiences spanning across thousands of decades. The Bible is also a book of commands, instructions, and precepts – a book of prescribed rules we must follow. It's important for us to take time to turn the pages of this book daily; searching the scriptures for information on what we should do and the ways in which we should go. We need to knock on the doors of the sixty-six books in the Bible so that they can reveal the goodness that they have for us, the instructions and the precepts that God has ordered us to follow in order to benefit ourselves and those around us.

Every time you seek the scriptures, you seek God. Every time you read God's word and meditate, ponder, or reason within your heart and mind, you're seeking God. Every time you seek God through His word, you love Him.

2. Seeking God through Prayer

"For I know the thoughts that I think toward you, says the Lord, thoughts of peace and not of evil, to give you a future and a hope. Then you will call upon Me and go and pray to Me, and I will listen to you. And you will seek Me and find Me, when you search for Me with all your heart."   —*Jeremiah 29:11–13*

Prayer is simply talking to God. God is our heavenly Father, we can ask Him whatever we want, whenever we want, wherever we are. There comes a time during our private conversations with God when He wants us to ask Him the question, "Father, what is your will?" Commandments are written *and* spoken. They are spoken to you directly from your heavenly Father Himself, and they are spoken daily – in your heart, your mind, and your spirit.

When we speak to God, He speaks back to us. When we ask Him certain questions, we receive certain answers. When we talk to Him about the steps that we should take and seek His direction, He shows us the way to go. When we seek His commands concerning areas of our lives or situations that we're going through, He reveals His plans and precepts for us (by letting us know what to do and how to do it).

> When you pray, you seek God. Every time you ask Him about His will, you seek God. Every time you ask for His commands, you seek God. Every time that you talk and converse with God, you love Him.

3. Seeking God through Worship

"With my whole heart I have sought You; oh, let me not wander from Your commandments!" —*Psalm 119:10*

Reading your Bible, spending time in prayer, and singing a song of complete surrender to God – These things are all forms of worship. Whenever we engage our hearts towards God, we engage in worship. Worship is a lifestyle that seeks to please God. Worship is more than a song, yet we can worship through song. We worship God with songs written by others, and we worship God by birthing a new song in our spirits. We worship God with words on our lips and songs in our hearts. When we worship through song, we should seek God, His will, and His way. Let us worship with minds and hearts that are ready and willing to receive His commands in our cores. God desires us to seek Him with all that is within us – with our hearts, our minds, and our souls. Seeking God is the first step in obeying and loving God.

"But from there you will seek the Lord your God, and you will find Him if you seek Him with all your heart and with all your soul." —*Deuteronomy 4:29*

"The Lord looks down from heaven upon the children of men, to see if there are any who understand, who seek God."—*Psalm 14:2*

"See, I have set before you today life and good, death and evil, in that I command you today to love the Lord your God, to walk in His ways, and to keep His commandments, His statutes, and His judgments, that you may live and multiply; and the Lord your God will bless you in the land which you go to possess." —*Deuteronomy 30:15–16*

Seek to know Him; seek to understand Him; seek to know His will for you; seek to follow His ways; seek to obey Him; seek to please Him; seek to love Him.

Now Put It in Action

After seeking and attaining His commandments, we have to act on them. This is where the Holy Spirit and His grace come into play. The commands of God are to be kept and held fast once received. We are to keep them carefully within ourselves and never let go of them; we are to fulfil His commands for us through obedience, by carrying out what He's asked us to do.

Though the commandments of God are beneficial to us, they are not always easy to exercise. In fact, they can be pretty uncomfortable to execute. When we apply the grace of God to the instruction of God, we can fulfil our love for God. That's how He wants it, so that's how we should give it. When we obey God, we start the fulfilment of our love relationship with God, and we establish the first stage in the building of our concrete soul substruction with the mixing of our agape cement.

CHAPTER 9

Loving Me, Loving You

"And the second is like it: 'You shall love your neighbour as yourself.'"
— *Matthew 22:39*

Loving Me, Loving You

It's very easy to read Matthew 22:39 and say, "God wants me to love Him and then start loving you." And after a quick read, it looks like that's what Jesus was saying. Let's take some time to dissect the instruction in this text, though, so that we can gain a clear understanding of what God is actually asking us to do. We are to love our neighbours as ourselves. It's very clear that we need to love others, but what isn't so clear is that we need to love ourselves before attempting to love others. A lot of times, we attempt to be givers of love even though we lack authentic love for ourselves. Love was designed to function properly and effectively through a divine and strategic process.

It's designed in such a way that, once you've started the process of loving God with all of your heart, mind, and soul, the next thing to do is to love yourself. The process of loving yourself authentically is the final step in the mixing of your cement of agape love, which will finalise the building process of your foundation.

In receiving this insight through my search to re-establish myself, I had to ask myself the following questions: *Do I know or even understand the process and the way in which I'm meant to authentically love myself? Do I love myself?* I wasn't sure. I knew that I was pleased with my physical features and that I took care of myself, but I wasn't completely sure whether I truly loved myself in the way that agape love wanted me to. The way to resolve the conflict was to find out how God wanted me to love myself. I found the answer, and it was clear. God wanted me to love myself in love. That's right: God wanted me to love myself in *love*.

Knowing God; Knowing Love

When you seek God, you seek love because God *is* love. It's in 1 John 4:7–8 that we receive the revelation that God is actually the source of love, and that, in knowing God, we can know the meaning of authentic love.

"Beloved, let us love one another, for love is of God; and everyone who loves is born of God and knows God. He who does not love does not know God, for God is love."   *—1 John 4:7–8*

God is the very source of love. His being is love, His existence is love, and He is the very essence of love. God is authentic love, and authentic love is God. Not knowing God equals not experiencing authentic love. To have authentic love, you first have to be born of God and know Him. In order for us to really love ourselves, we need to get in love; we need to be born of love. It's important for us to understand the wisdom in the processing order of love because it's when we follow the first step in the order that we actually get to the point of knowing God.

When we receive Jesus Christ as our Lord and Saviour, we become born-again, which makes us reborn of love because Christ *is* Love. But being born-again doesn't make you knowledgeable. The act of becoming born-again (through your repentance of sin and your acceptance of Jesus Christ) causes you to be accepted into the body of Christ and the family of God, which is the family of Love. This wonderful process doesn't automatically endow you with complete knowledge of God, though. But by following the first and greatest commandment of loving God with all of your heart, soul, and mind, you attain the knowledge of who God is. It's in your daily seeking of God via the Bible, in prayer, in worship, and in fasting that you place yourself in a position where you can really know God. You can then receive His love fully. Let's look at John 14:21 and John 15:9–12:

"He who has My commandments and keeps them, it is he who loves Me. And he who loves Me will be loved by My Father, and I will love him and manifest Myself to him."   —*John 14:21*

"As the Father loved Me, I also have loved you; abide in My love. If you keep My commandments, you will abide in My love, just as I have kept My Father's commandments and abide in His love. "These things I have spoken to you, that My joy may remain in you, and that your joy may be full. This is My commandment, that you love one another as I have loved you."   —*John 15:9–12*

It's Like Being Baked in an Oven

In both scriptures, the point is made very clearly: when we love God as He wants us to love Him, He will love us fully. When we rightly position ourselves in our hearts, minds, and souls to love God truly, He pours His love on us. John 14:21 says, "And he who loves Me will be loved by My Father, and I will love him and *manifest* Myself to him." This is a wonderful piece of scripture. The picture in this verse is just beautiful because it tells us that when we love God as we really ought to, God loves us (and God the Son loves in us). We are loved on by The Father to the extent that the love of our Messiah is manifested in us. Until He manifests Himself in you, you can never truly love yourself as you were designed to.

You're going to have to give God all the room that He needs in order for Him to love you as He desires to love you. The way we give God room to love us is by seeking God's will and saying *yes* to His commands for us, emptying ourselves of our own will and saying yes to His divine will. Once you say *yes* to Him, the room is open, His manifestation takes effect, and you are changed. Once you allow God the room to love you as He really wants to, it's important that you stay in that posture so that you don't disrupt the flow of His love in you. Jesus says in John 15:9, "Abide in My love." He's telling us to continue to be present and dwell in the fullness of His love.

We all need to make seeking and pleasing God an everyday part of life. We need to pray for the supernatural grace of God to obey His will. We need to pray for this because the reality of desiring, seeking, and obeying God isn't always easy. We're human, and sometimes our human nature doesn't feel like pleasing God. That's life. But because we know how life is, we know that we have to tap into the wisdom of prayer; we need to pray so that we can reside in the fullness of His love. When you make room for God, He will fill you up with His love.

Most of us have experienced some type of love, but a lot of us haven't experienced love in its full measure. It takes a certain measure of love to love yourself as God desires you to love. This measure manifests when you are willing to receive it. I know this to be true because, even as a born-again Christian, I wasn't experiencing love in its fullness. It was only when I started seeking God with all of my heart, mind, and soul (through prayer, reading the Bible, and worshipping) that I started feeling a change within myself. It was like a warming sensation that illuminated the core of my being and the centre of my heart. I started feeling feelings within myself that I had never experienced before. I couldn't properly explain it, but I understood what it was: the authentic love of the Father through the love of His Son. It was real, and it was awesome. I felt the fullness of God Himself. All the residue from the shame that I had encountered, the disgrace that I endured, and the pains that I suffered were gently but thoroughly being washed away from my heart, my soul, and my mind.

God loved on and in me, and in turn, I was automatically and with total ease loving myself. My self-perception changed; I saw myself the way God saw me and appreciated what He appreciated in me. I loved myself in the same way that He loved me, and I gave Him room so He could love me completely. All the times I was seeking God, He was loving me, and all the times I was obeying God, He was loving me. The process of loving myself first started when I started loving God. When I got in the oven of love, the heat of love got in me.

Developing a Character of Love

The process of loving yourself authentically through the love of God doesn't just change how you think or feel, but also your character. To know love and love yourself is to embrace the fruit of the Spirit:

"But the fruit of the Spirit is love, joy, peace, longsuffering, kindness, goodness, faithfulness, gentleness, self-control. Against such there is no law."   —*Galatians 5:22–23*

The fruit of the Spirit is the choice of the Spirit. The fruit of the Spirit can also be viewed as the values or the character of the Holy Spirit. The character of the Spirit starts off with love, and everything that follows is related to love.

Understand the Values of Love

Joy

Love presents joy as a value that produces cheerfulness, a calm and internal delight. One can be full of joy or exceedingly joyful.

Peace

Love presents peace as a value because of the state that it puts a person or a group of people in. To have peace or to be at peace is to be in a state of tranquillity, quietness, stillness, and rest. Peace makes us exempt from rage, even amid chaos and confusion. Peace among individuals brings about a harmony, a smooth functioning. Peace brings about safety and security, ensuring that things are kept well. To value peace is to value prosperity.

Long-Suffering

Love presents long-suffering as a value because it produces patience, constancy, endurance, steadfastness, perseverance, forbearance, and fortitude.

Kindness

Love presents kindness as a value because of the moral, virtuous goodness that it births within us. It is a pleasant gentleness. To value kindness is to value moral excellence.

Goodness

Love presents goodness as a value because it displays the uprightness of one's heart.

Faithfulness

Love presents faithfulness as a value because it indicates a moral conviction, the acceptance of truth. You can rely on faithfulness because it will believe in you, agree with you, assure you, and have confidence in you. Faithfulness is a value of love because it is "in it" for the long haul.

Gentleness

Love presents gentleness of spirit as a value because of the mildness of its disposition and its strength. Gentleness is humility and meekness. To value the gentleness of humility is to value the quietness of power and strength.

Self-Control

Love presents self-control as a value because it is the virtue of one who masters his or her desires, feelings, and passions. It is the ability to control yourself in all areas of your life.

The fruit of the Spirit shouldn't be viewed only as the values or the character of the Spirit, but also as the state and the environment that it creates for an individual within himself or herself. The fruit of the Spirit as a whole surrounds, conditions, and sets us in an internal environment of nothing but that which is beneficial for our hearts, souls, and minds. It places us in a state of cheerful internal security while securing us from external hostile environments. The fruit of the Spirit keeps us in a loving environment that allows us to operate and function in the way of love. As you receive the values of love, it will create the second layer of the concrete substruction of your soul. All eight values and characteristics of love create the concrete, rock-like strength of agape love.

Once you've attained the character of love, no matter what your temperament is, you will always be defined as a quality person with a lovely personality. As your character gets renewed and established in the love and the character of God, your personality will get renewed, too. Whether you're an extrovert or introvert, your personality will become more pleasant because it stems from authentic love in Christ Jesus, which carries a presence of love within it. Loving yourself in the fullness of Christ's love for you won't change your temperament, but it will establish a new substruction of God-loving values and virtues that will prepare you for life and make you a remarkable person.

Once you're in a position of love, having a loveable character and a loveable personality, you'll be in the right position to effectively and correctly love your neighbour as yourself.

> Love yourself and become your own friend.

CHAPTER 10

The Friend of Friendship

In Order to Be, You First Have to Become

"A man who has friends must himself be friendly, but there is a friend who sticks closer than a brother."   *—Proverbs 18:24*

Being a friend is just as important as gaining a friend. If you're going to be a lifelong friend, confidant, and companion to someone other than yourself, you're going to have to become all that a friend can be. When you look at the root meaning of friendship in its original form (in the biblical scriptures), you get words such as *to shepherd, teacher, tend, pasture, graze,* and *feed.* In order to be a person with the authentic qualities of a true friend, you have to take on the same nature of a good shepherd. After all, a true friend cares for his or her friend just as a good shepherd cares for the flock.

To tend to someone is to direct them to a certain place. Good shepherds do this all the time. They constantly direct their sheep towards greener and better pastures. The green pastures supply succulent, herbaceous vegetation from which the sheep get nourishment and strength. Sheep need good and rich pastures to survive. It is in the green pastures that shepherds observe their flocks. A good shepherd cares for the flock by managing, watching, and protecting them. A really good friend will direct his or her friend to greener pastures by directing him or her to good places. A friend will feed his or her friend with good advice and watch out for any threats to that friend.

It's only by the grace of God, which flows through His love and His wisdom, that you can possess the qualities and attributes of an authentic friend. Without His love and wisdom, it will be difficult to be a very good friend. When the love and wisdom of God is within you, being a friend to yourself and others may not always be easy, but it will always be natural. When the love and wisdom of God is within you – even when you're in a bad mood – you will be able to be a good friend to someone else.

The House of Friendship

God created you for relationships. God wants you to excel in your relationships. He wants you to excel in your relationship with Him, your relationship with yourself, and your relationship with your spouse. This is because your friendships are mental, emotional, and spiritual houses that have been designed by God to keep the grounds of your emotions and thoughts protected. The most important part of the friendship is the thing that it consists of: the individuals. When entering into a friendship with someone else, you're automatically taking on the responsibility and role of a builder who's working to create a strong friendship house. Apart from yourself, the most important things you will invest in are your relationships.

Becoming a friend to someone else is a choice before it is anything else. You have to be rational when faced with the choice of entering into a friendship. You have to be wise, prudent, and discerning. Because you're aiming to be a worthy friend to someone else, you need to make sure that you're entering into a friendship with someone who is aiming to be a God-ordained friend to you, too. If only one person possesses the divine qualities of a friend, a true friendship cannot be established. When all individuals possess the divine qualities of a friend, authentic friendship may be established.

Established through Covenant

Amos 3:3 says, "Can two walk together, unless they are agreed?" In other words, can two people build a friendship or relationship unless they are in agreement with one another? No. You have to choose your friendships and relationships wisely – unless you are both united via a covenant, you cannot be true friends. It's one thing to possess the qualities of an authentic friend, and it's another thing to know who is worthy of becoming a lifelong friend. You are called on to love everybody, but you shouldn't invest in the lives of everybody. Being friendly is not the same as being a friend.

There is true value in a true friend, and there is true value in that friendship. It is important for you to understand that friendship is not based solely on the qualities of a person; it is based on his or her goals and desires for both of you in your friendship house. A *you* and a *me* do not always equal a *we,* but a *we* always equals the sum of *you and me together.* Establishing the covenant in *we* will establish your relationship and friendship in the lifelong house of marriage – your agreement in your convent establishes your *we.*

Life Is Better When It Is Shared with the Right Person

Ecclesiastes 4:9–12 is a great piece of scripture for explaining the benefits of having a true friendship with a true friend:

> *"Two are better than one,*
> *Because they have a good reward for their labor.*
> *For if they fall, one will lift up his companion.*
> *But woe to him who is alone when he falls,*
> *For he has no one to help him up.*

Again, if two lie down together, they will keep warm;
But how can one be warm alone?
Though one may be overpowered by another, two can withstand him.
And a threefold cord is not quickly broken."

"Two are better than one." The word *better* in this passage is the same word for *good* in Genesis 2:18: "And the Lord God said, 'It is not good that man should be alone; I will make him a helper comparable to him.'" The words *better* and *good* mean *well, beautiful, bountiful, cheerful,* and *prosperous.* Better is good, and good is better. It's not good for man to be alone, because two are better than one.

Remember: "They have a good reward for their labor." The word *reward* originally translated to *existence.* When you join yourself to the right person, you receive a good existence. When you join in a friendship, a covenant, and a partnership with your lifelong friend and spouse, you live a better life, creating and experiencing a better reality. As you stand in a lifelong agreement with your spouse, even while you struggle through troubles, heartache, pain, and worries, you'll see your reality get better sooner or later. At the end of it all, the two of you will create a better reality than you ever could have imagined. This is because, in friendship, there is unity. Look at it like this: the existence of your friend determines your existence, and the reality of your life determines your friend's reality. Why? Because you're both knitted together mentally, emotionally, and spiritually. When the other hurts, you feel that hurt. When you ache, the other feels that pain. Your well-being affects the other's well-being. When one falls, the other will pick him or her up. When the fallen has a friend, he or she has a hope because, in that friend, there is always help to get back up again. Two are better than one at all times, even when you fall down together. It is extremely bad when a person falls alone; a person who falls alone is in a hopeless situation. That person's reality is filled with grief and despair. He or she can cry out, but no true friend will attend to the cry.

A true friend is more precious than pure silver, and authentic friendship is more valuable than pure gold. Invest in the housing market of friendship wisely, and make sure that you purchase your friendships using love and wisdom. The house of your God-given friendship in marriage will make your existence better. Indeed, it is not good for man to be alone; two are better than one.

My Prayer for You

I pray that the process I've described will take effect immediately in your life. I pray that, when you decide to face the reality of your past and your present, you will do so with the grace and the comfort of the precious Holy Spirit. I pray that, as you cry throughout your process, He will dry your tears. I pray that, as you hurt throughout your process, the Holy Spirit will heal you; as you embark on the process of becoming a quality person, you will become totally sand free in every area of your life. I pray that, as you leave the old to embrace the new, the quality of your life will reach great heights. Because you've decided to become a better person, I pray that you will become a quality individual, a quality friend, and a quality spouse in the future. I also pray that you will join yourself in agreement and in covenant with a spouse of the highest quality. By the grace of God, in His love and through His wisdom, you will never be the same again. I declare that you are now whole, 100 per cent complete in your disposition, your heart, and your soul. In Christ's mighty name, I pray. Amen.

About the Book

Everybody wants to be happy, everybody wants to be loved, and everybody wants to be treated well. Every single person wants to be with someone who will treat him or her with respect and honour. Every single person wants to be with a person of great quality. But nobody seems to be focusing on becoming an individual of great quality within his or her *own* mindset.

Love is so much more than a feeling or sensation; love is a way of thinking, a way of acting, and a type of character. Too often, we want things from people without attempting to gain for ourselves what we want from them. It's one thing to find somebody who will love you well, and it's another thing to be someone who will love his or her partner well too. You might be looking to enter into a relationship, but you might not be ready yet.

Love and Wisdom is more than just a book; it's a reality check and a reality guide. It will help you re-establish your reality so that you can eventually enjoy a loving relationship with another loving person.

Printed in the United States
By Bookmasters